SPIRITUAL MESSAGES FOR WOMEN

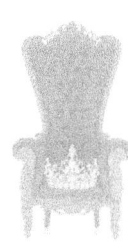

With a Crown and No Home

Spiritual Messages for Women

SPIRITUAL MESSAGES FOR WOMEN

With a Crown and No Home

SPIRITUAL MESSAGES FOR WOMEN

ONEDIA NICOLE GAGE, PH. D., CLC

DEDICATION

FOR EVERY WOMAN WHO SEEKS HER CROWN

FOR EVERY WOMAN WHO IS TRYING TO ABANDON HER CROWN

FOR EVERY WOMAN WHO IS EMOTIONALLY HOMELESS

FOR EVERY WOMAN WHO IS MENTALLY FRAZZLED

FOR EVERY WOMAN WHO IS SPIRITUALLY CHALLENGED

WOMEN, SOMETIMES WE WEAR OUR CROWN AND HAVE NO HOME

I PRAY THAT THESE MESSAGES BRING YOU TO A BETTER SPIRITUAL PEACE

AND PROVIDES YOU WITH THE CONFIDENCE TO ADJUST THAT CROWN SO THAT WEARING IT IS EASIER TO EMBRACE.

Scriptures

Genesis 1:27
²⁷So God created mankind in his own image,
in the image of God he created them;
male and female he created them.

Proverbs 18:22
²²He who finds a wife finds what is good
and receives favor from the Lord.

Matthew 11:28
²⁸ "Come to me, all you who are weary and burdened, and I will
give you rest.

Library of Congress

With a Crown and No Home:
Spiritual Messages for Women

All Rights Reserved © 2025

Onedia N. Gage, Ph. D., CLC

No part of this book may be reproduced or transmitted in
Any form or by any means, graphic, electronic, or mechanical,
Including photocopying, recording, taping, or by any
Information storage or retrieval system, without the
Permission in writing from the publisher.

Purple Ink, Inc. Press

For Information address:
Purple Ink, Inc.
1202 E. 1st St., 14931,
Humble, TX 77347
www.purpleink.net ♦ onediagage@purpleink.net

Onedia Gage Speaks

www.onediagespeaks.com ♦
onediagage@onediagespeaks.com

ISBN:

978-1-939119-84-1

Printed in the United States

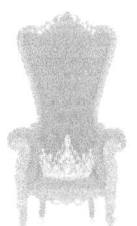

Other Books by
Onedia N. Gage, Ph. D., CLC

Are You Ready for 9th Grade . . . Again? A Family's Guide to Success
As We Grow Together Daily Devotional for Expectant Couples
As We Grow Together Prayer Journal for Expectant Couples
As We Grow Together Bible Study: Her Workbook
As We Grow Together Bible Study: His Workbook
Because I Do: A Working Marriage—Her Workbook
Because I Do: A Working Marriage—His Workbook
The Best 40 Days of My Life: A Journey of Spiritual Renewal
The Blue Print: Poetry for the Soul
From Fat to Fit in 90 Days: A Fitness Journal
From Two to One: The Notebook for the Christian Couple
Hannah's Voice: Powerful Lessons in Prayer
The Heart of a Woman: The Depth of Her Soul
Her Story The Legacy of Her Fight: The Bible Study
Her Story The Legacy of Her Fight: The Devotional
Her Story The Legacy of Her Fight: The Legacy Journal
Her Story The Legacy of Her Fight: Prayers and Journal
I Am.: 90 Days of Powerful Words: Affirmation and Advice for Girls
ily! A Mother-Daughter Relationship Workbook
In 90 Days: What Will You Do?
In Her Own Words: Notebook for the Christian Woman
In Purple Ink: Poetry for the Spirit
In Your Hands: A Dad's Impact on His Daughter's Self-Esteem
Intensive Couples Retreat: Her Workbook
Intensive Couples Retreat: His Workbook
Living A Whole Life: Sermons Which Prompt, Provoke, and Provide Life
Living An Authentic Life
Love Letters to God from a Teenage Girl
The Measure of a Woman: The Details of Her Soul
The Notebook: For Me, About Me, By Me
The Notebook for the Christian Teen
On the Same Team
On This Journey Daily Devotional for Young People
On This Journey Prayer Journal for Young People
On This Journey Prayer Journal for Young People, Vol. 2
One Day More Than We Deserve Prayer Journal for the Growing Christian
Promises, Promises: A Christian Novel

Queen in the Making: 30-Week Bible Study for Teen Girls
Queen in the Making: 30 Week Bible Study for Teen Girls Leader's Guide
The Secrets of My Success: Business Coaching How does she do it? Who does she think she is?
Serve the Staff: The Impact of a Healthy Social-Emotional Climate and Culture
She Spoke Volumes . . . And Then Some
Six Months of Solitude: The Sanctity of Singleness Notebook
Six Months of Solitude: The Sanctity of Singleness Prayers and Journal
There's a Queen Within: Her Journey to Building Self—Worth
Tools for These Times: Timely Sermons for Uncertain Times
The Vision Notebook
Walking Tall with a Broken Life
What Did You Say?: Affirmations. Encouragement. Motivation.
With a Crown and No Home
With An Anointed Voice: The Power of Prayer
A Woman Like Me: A Bible Study for Women to Survive Our Times
A Woman Like Me: A Daily Devotional for Women to Survive Our Times
A Woman Like Me: A Sermonic Study Lessons for Us Women
Yielded and Submitted: A Woman's Journey for a Life Dedicated to God
Yielded and Submitted: A Woman's Journey for a Life Dedicated to God An Intimate Study
Yielded and Submitted: A Woman's Journey for a Life Dedicated to God Prayers and Journal

The Nehemiah Character Series

Nehemiah and His Basketball
Nehemiah and His Big Sister
Nehemiah and His Bike
Nehemiah and His Flag Football Team
Nehemiah and His Football
Nehemiah and His Golf Clubs
Nehemiah and Math
Nehemiah and the Bully
Nehemiah and the Busy Day
Nehemiah and the Class Field Trip
Nehemiah and the Substitute for the Substitute

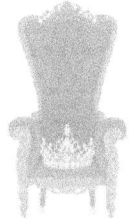

Nehemiah Can Swim
Nehemiah Found the Mud
Nehemiah Reads to Mommy
Nehemiah Writes Just Like Mommy
Nehemiah, the Hot Dog, and the Broccoli
Nehemiah's Family Vacation
Nehemiah's Favorite Teacher Returns to School
Nehemiah's First Day of School
Nehemiah's Sister Moved
Nehemiah's Visit to the Hospital

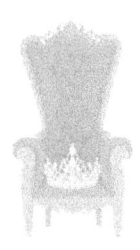

Dear God,

Thank you for giving us a Crown and the direction for what to do with this Crown. We appreciate your faith in us with this Crown. We are hopeful that we can fulfill every promise and every duty in order to make you proud of who made us to be.

I thank you for these messages. In them, I have found solace. The title of the book is a place of hurt for me. I thank you for salvaging me in these messages me.

You give the messenger the message first and I had to deal with my own issues first. I thank you for that as well. This project meant something different this time.

I just live to make you proud so I hope that I am doing a good job.

Thank you for these messages. I cannot wait to see the results of Your work.

Sincerely,

Onedia N. Gage

SPIRITUAL MESSAGES FOR WOMEN

Dear Crown Wearers and Those Who are Afraid of that Crown:

I am the Queen with the Crown with No Home. While it seems prophetic, I am the poster woman for not being accepted in places that I want to love. I have to tell this story all of the time. I have been homeless actually. I have been professionally homeless. I have a homeless heart. After I say all of that, you may wonder how can I even muster enough emotional energy to author this book.

I do so because you are going to read this and hopefully it will change your life. I have lived what is on these pages and have grown from it tremendously. I hope that you grow as well.

I know that my road ahead has lots of work but I have to count it all joy in the outcome of that labor.

I wish that you are at your best self on this journey. Send me your testimony. onediagage@onediagagespeaks.com.

Wear the Crown! With an upright head and heart! Hold your head up. The Crown needs a platform.

Sincerely,

Onedia N. Gage

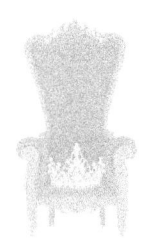

Table of Contents

Prayer

Letter to the Crown Wearers

The Mirror: Can You See Your Crown?

Genesis 1:27

25

A New Home, A New Crown

Esther 2:17

29

Teach Me to Wear the Crown: A Legacy Worth Living

Ruth 1:8—18

33

The Crown Has Wisdom: Wisdom Is as Wisdom Does

Titus 2:1—5

39

The Crown Has Worth

Spiritual Messages for Women

Proverbs 31:10—14

43

The Crown Works

Proverbs 31:15—20

49

The Crown Is

Proverbs 31:21—26

55

The Crown's Work

Proverbs 31:27—31

61

God's GPS for The Crown

Proverbs 18:22

65

The Crown Has Standards: What Time is Your Flight

John 8:32

69

The Crown Decides Priorities

Luke 10:38—41

73

The Crown Rests

Matthew 11:28

77

The Crown's Extravagance

1 Corinthians 13:13b MSG

81

The Crown Has Wrath: Keep Your Wits about You

Ephesians 4:26—27

85

The Crown has Faith

Hebrews 11:6

89

Resources   93

Acknowledgements   95

SPIRITUAL MESSAGES FOR WOMEN

About the Crown Wearer   97

Book the Crown Wearer   99

With a Crown and No Home

THE MIRROR:

CAN YOU SEE YOUR CROWN?

> [27] So God created mankind in His own image,
> in the image of God He created them;
> male and female He created them.
>
> Genesis 1:27

"Mirror, mirror on the wall, who is the fairest of them all?" These famous words have been uttered millions of times when we read the fairy tale, "Snow White and the Seven Dwarfs." The wicked queen asked this question daily. Daily, the mirror will declare that she was indeed the fairest. In this context, fairest was defined as the most beautiful.

Well one day, the mirror changed his response to Snow White. The wicked queen was more than disgusted. She was so angry. That anger led to more wickedness; to the point where the wicked queen tried to kill Snow White.

The mirror is a powerful tool, but mostly you use it against yourself. Have you looked at the mirror lately without being critical? I mean not mentally making the eyebrow arching appointment or the hair appointment or the facial appointment. Not when you're taking those beautiful car selfies or desk selfies. I want you to consider looking at the mirror without criticizing your nose or your forehead or your lash length. I mean look at yourself with the eyes of your Creator.

He created you, along with that forehead, lash length, hair texture, hair behavior, nose width, eye color, and all the other attributes we frequently criticize. But what we are really doing is telling God that He is not doing a good job and put together a bad product: you. When in fact that's not actually the case at all.

Have you ever considered how you sound when you say, 'my forehead is huge!'? No, you don't actually. However, we are made according to God's wishes. We are not the author of ourselves, yet we are the harshest critics of ourselves.

When we look at ourselves and make these impossible suggestions, can you see your Crown in that mirror?

Did you ask what Crown? That is a great question. You have a Crown. God created you a Queen. In the world where we live, all Queens wear Crowns or they will. You may not wear one every day visibly, but your invisible one is there daily.

Can you see that Crown? Is it up right? Perfectly? Tilted to one side or the other? Too far front? Too far back? Is it too small? Too big? What other critiques are there?

What is wrong with that Crown? Leave it alone. Stop touching it. Stop looking at it with such harsh eyes. Stop.

You are made in the image of God. God is not a Queen but instead a King. He is a Creator. Before now, did you know it? If so, do you see your Crown?

Why is this Crown important? The location of the Crown is indicative of the location of your head's posture. If your head is down, then your Crown is in the full view as well as your hair. Your Crown should be held high because your head will be high and upright.

The position of your head is also the position of your heart; all of this is the disposition of your self-esteem. In His Image translates into your emotional well-being. When you are not doing well, how does that reflect on God?

Your Crown is your representation of your attitude about yourself. Is that a good position that you find yourself in? If not, what is your plan to be able to return to the Crown that you need in order to stand tall for yourself.

When you look in the mirror, can you make yourself some promises about your future? This starts with recognizing yourself as a whole person. There are not pieces of you. There is just the whole you. That whole you needs love and affirmation, care and concern.

Consider stepping out of your own way. You are the reason that you don't achieve some things. You talk yourself out of trying quite a few goals and dreams. You don't have to use your fear to stop you from trying to be all that you can be.

Promise yourself that you will continue learning both formally and informally. Remind yourself that you are valuable. That you have worth. That you can see the phenom that you are.

He made you in His image. He used some great details to put you together. He did not make a mess. He did not make a mistake. Start looking for your Crown in the mirror. Start affirming yourself because you do not need to rest your chin on your chest. That 90° angle needs to be maintained and cared for, affirmed and uplifted.

Watch that Crown. It may need adjusting from time to time. It may need to be removed from maintenance, for polishing or tightening. Wear that Crown. Proudly. With everything that you will wear.

Keep focus on the work so that we can keep the Crown.

Look for the Crown intentionally, intently. It is there and it will be always.

A New Crown, A New Home

> ¹⁷ Now the King was attracted to Esther more than to any of the other women, and she won his favor and approval more than any of the other virgins. So he set a royal Crown on her head and made her Queen instead of Vashti.
>
> Esther 2:17

Transition is difficult enough, but for a woman to become a Queen overnight at a new home, with new rules, roles and traditions, and without family, it is next to impossible.

Esther became Queen. Overnight. Through an interesting selection process. Queen was a role that she never anticipated. She never even wanted the job.

The previous Queen had difficulties with the King, so he ousted her. As was their tradition, the King looked for a new Queen. The process is one such that after the King meets and interviews the prospect, she is no longer able to go into regular society. That is a huge risk for the lady that meets him, but it is also a great opportunity; one that will never happen again.

In this story, Esther is a special situation: her cousin works for the King. He shares 'inside information' with her. She uses that information then becomes Queen. Imagine that life! Queen!

Queens have servants, new family, new friends, and upgraded status, and a platform. This new Crown provides her with a stage to help others, to improve conditions, to make policy changes, and to contribute to the softer side of the King and the Kingdom.

A new home is also part of this new Crown. Esther probably did not understand until a few years into her role what she could do with the palace. She had the opportunity to put her own spin on the location.

Esther was introduced to the whole new lifestyle. She now had maid servants and a staff to manage. What an undertaking! When we as women get a new position or move to a new location, we must consider the job ahead of us. We do not always know what we will face, or what we need to know so that we can overcome the obstacle. This confidence does have its issues but these issues are surely details that we can overcome. This requires work from time to time. But if we do not have to address any additional issues, then we need to be grateful. Consider the changes that we have endured. Compare the changes to that of Esther's life. Keep in mind that these changes also require us to grow and mature. This growth includes learning more about your new role. In Esther's case, she would need to learn about her husband, her new culture, and her environment. This is no small feat.

Focus on the main details: the new Crown. You may ask yourself why you were chosen. You may want to consider what you need to be successful. Who will you need to help you to be successful?

Esther had her cousin, Mordecai. He was instrumental in her becoming Queen and now he would be helpful in her being successful in her role as Queen.

It is time to set goals in this new role. This goal is meaningful and will require some work. As we enter new places and begin functioning in new roles, we must address our personal deficiencies and maximize our personal strengths. The goal requires full immersion yourself into the role so that you will extend your territory.

After goal setting, then you need to work on your image for this new role. New Crown equals new you. Let's change our hair, our dress, our activities, and add some new associates. This is a time to expand your reach, your influence, and your thoughts. These changes will establish you as a game changer.

This new role will require some new ideas and new practices. This role will forever change your life so, how do you make this life changing role the best gig of your life?

If there was ever a time to make sure that you contribute to the lives of others and to make a huge impact on your community, then the time is now.

This will be the hardest thing that you have ever achieved. It will require the most of you and the best of you. More than you have ever given, if you plan to be successful.

You are not the first person this has ever happened to, so we have proof that you can be successful. Your life is now on display and serves as an example to other women and young women of what is possible.

This is a great time to discard old habits and unsafe practices; forgive yourself for your past in its entirety. Give yourself permission to be great, to be awesome, and to have a huge impact on others. The same impact that someone had on you when you needed guidance and mentorship.

Make sure that this new chapter lives up to the expectation of such a level. This level is not without its tasks and maybe a few difficulties, but you need to approach that challenge with grace and fortitude.

A new Crown and A new home.

Teach Me to Wear the Crown:

A Legacy Worth Living

⁸ Then Naomi said to her two daughters-in-law, "Go back, each of you, to your mother's home. May the Lord show you kindness, as you have shown kindness to your dead husbands and to me. ⁹ May the Lord grant that each of you will find rest in the home of another husband."

Then she kissed them goodbye and they wept aloud ¹⁰ and said to her, "We will go back with you to your people."

¹¹ But Naomi said, "Return home, my daughters. Why would you come with me? Am I going to have any more sons, who could become your husbands? ¹² Return home, my daughters; I am too old to have another husband. Even if I thought there was still hope for me—even if I had a husband tonight and then gave birth to sons— ¹³ would you wait until they grew up? Would you remain unmarried for them? No, my daughters. It is more bitter for me than for you, because the Lord's hand has turned against me!"

¹⁴ At this they wept aloud again. Then Orpah kissed her mother-in-law goodbye, but Ruth clung to her.

¹⁵ "Look," said Naomi, "your sister-in-law is going back to her people and her gods. Go back with her."

¹⁶ But Ruth replied, "Don't urge me to leave you or to turn back from you. Where you go I will go, and where you stay I will stay. Your people will be my people and your God my God. ¹⁷ Where you die I will die, and there I will be buried. May the Lord deal with me, be it ever so severely, if even death

separates you and me." ¹⁸ When Naomi realized that Ruth was determined to go with her, she stopped urging her.

Ruth 1:8-18

Naomi was married but she became a widow because of a war. This war also killed her sons, the husbands of Ruth and Orpah. After the dust settled, Naomi advised her daughters-in-law to go back to their homes and to leave her. Naomi was probably depressed and uncertain about her worth, upset about her circumstances, and feeling worthless. We have all been in that seat.

Ruth listened intently. At the close of Naomi's announcement, Ruth said no. Ruth said absolutely not. Ruth said the most eloquent and profound statement ever: "Where you go, I will go. Where you stay, I will stay." This statement took over Naomi's soul. She had no response. She could only say, 'Okay, let's go.' Naomi took Ruth back to her home for them to both live and recover their lives.

Naomi had probably never known her ultimate worth. Naomi was not a mentor but she never realized how her leadership and love made such a huge difference in Ruth's life. Naomi had to pull her own life together so that she could continue to lead and love. She never anticipated this type of push from Ruth. She was not prepared initially, but she soon realized that she was more valuable than she thought.

Boaz was wise. This wisdom cannot be bought or taught. This is God-given wisdom. Ruth was a next level woman - one that God created for His work.

Naomi and Ruth's return to Naomi's hometown. The culture and tradition is that the community takes care of widows. The culture and tradition dictate that someone marries these widows. Ruth learns the new environment and culture. Ruth embraced the culture.

Really, the deal was made for Boaz to pursue Ruth. Through the cultural connection, Boaz married Ruth.

Naomi stayed with Ruth as her mentor and advisor. Ruth focused on her perspective about life and her outcome was better than favorable. Consider Naomi. Do you have a Naomi or are you a Naomi? Both answers need to be yes. In this life, we need help. We need each other. There is a song called 'I Need You To Survive' by Hezekiah walker. The words are:

I need you. You need me. We are a part of God's body. Stand with me, agree with me. It is His will that every need be supplied. You are important to me. I need you to survive.

Stand with me.

Agree with me.

I pray for you.

You pray for me.

I love you.

I need you to survive.

I won't harm you with words form my mouth.

I need you to survive.

These are some of the most powerful words ever put together. The meaning of them is extremely powerful. And if we choose to love and live by and honor them, then we have changed. The respect between women needs to be upgraded. We need to end the 'every woman for herself, God for us all' mentality. Consider how you treat other women. Is it Godly, God-like? Is it pleasing to God? Are you okay with authentic love of another woman like Naomi and Ruth love each other? If not, why not? Is your self-esteem so low that you can't love someone else even though you don't love yourself? Why Don't You Love Yourself?

Invest in others. Let others invest in you. It may be painful initially but you need the investment. Other people need you to invest. The investment may not feel great initially but eventually you will grow personally and will help others to do the same.

This investment will be the best, most selfless act that you have ever participated in. This is more selfless than parenting because you are not related to the person by DNA. Giving of yourself is the full act of selflessness. This selflessness is a demonstration of what Jesus would do.

Naomi and Ruth's lives will forever be changed. Naomi taught Ruth how to wear the Crown even though we are not sure that Naomi realized that she was wearing a Crown as well. Naomi made sure that Ruth was worthy for her son. Naomi mentored her in all situations. Naomi was good to Ruth because she still wanted to be in her family after her husband died.
Naomi assisted them with a great family as they built and grew.

Ruth reminded Naomi that she was wearing a Crown. Naomi was downtrodden after the untimely, devastating death; however,

Ruth reminded her of her worth and her role. Who should you be helping with this matter? There should be at least one person who you can talk to about anything and her opinion garners respect and action. She ought to be able to call you to her and you respond by going to her, regardless of what you had been doing or were about to do.

Ruth let Naomi know that Ruth respected her and still needed her wisdom and leadership. Naomi had to comply. Ruth's announcement was firm and demonstrative of her love. Crowns do not have instructions attached. There are unwritten rules in every aspect of life. Naomi's role is to share the Crown rules with Ruth so that she can be successful as a Queen. You will not lose anything by sharing love in this manner.

Ruth was receptive to all of the wisdom that Naomi offered her. These two women created a legacy worth repeating in your life because they already lived theirs.

They produced the Legacy of a Crown.

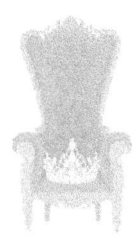

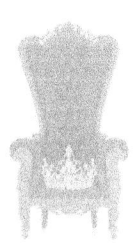

THE CROWN HAS WISDOM:

WISDOM IS AS WISDOM DOES

2 You, however, must teach what is appropriate to sound doctrine. ² Teach the older men to be temperate, worthy of respect, self-controlled, and sound in faith, in love and in endurance.

³ Likewise, teach the older women to be reverent in the way they live, not to be slanderers or addicted to much wine, but to teach what is good. ⁴ Then they can urge the younger women to love their husbands and children, ⁵ to be self-controlled and pure, to be busy at home, to be kind, and to be subject to their husbands, so that no one will malign the word of God.

Titus 2:1–5

Temperate. Grave. Solemn. Sober-minded. Sound in Faith. Love. Patience. Reverent in demeanor. Non-slanderer. Non-gossiper. Not too much wine. Teacher. Teacher of what is good. Training young women to love their husbands. Teaching them to love their children. Chaste. Entrepreneurs. Kind. Being subject to your husband. Honoring the word of God.

Lots of work? Not too much. Wisdom is involved in all of these characteristics. At first glance, we may consider it to be too much. But combined, these details define wisdom. Wisdom transforms how you live and how you treat others. Wisdom drives how you react. Wisdom grooms your behavior. Wisdom

helps you to think. Wisdom adjusts your attitude about your outlook. Wisdom facilitates your love for yourself. Wisdom ensures that you love others.

Wisdom needs no defense. Wisdom needs focus. Wisdom requires attentiveness. Witness influences purpose. Wisdom fills you. Wisdom makes you whole. Wisdom creates within you a new, clean heart. Wisdom uplifts your spirit. Wisdom delivers peace.

People wait their whole life in order to be considered wise, to be able to make good decisions, to be sought after for advice, and to be considered a person of treasure and legacy.

The Crown has wisdom. The Crown exercises wisdom. The Crown uses discretion. What does that look like? How will that be experienced? Let's investigate wisdom.

Wisdom is what happens when you bypass gossiping for guidance. When someone comes to gossip with you, rather than gossiping, you redirect them, then share with them how harmful it is to gossip. You may even suggest that they seek that person and speak to them directly about this matter.

Wisdom requires that we share with others what they need support with. Keep focused on the help and abandon the criticism. Remember that we all have shortcomings and there is a plank in your eye too. Imagine a woman who is helped by a wise woman who puts the other woman's needs above her own so that the woman can lift her head, so that she can believe again, and see some semblance of hope.

Wisdom speaks life into others so that they may live a life that they can learn to be proud of.

Women need wisdom in order to make good choices. These choices affect a generation and a legacy. These decisions that we make as a family, leader, a matriarch, are ones that others will benefit from or be sacrificed by for the rest of their lives. Poor and absent matriarchy is the root of the most of our problems in the world. A woman dictates the climate, future, and legacy of a family. Your family and community need you to be wise and to share that wisdom.

Women also need to have a wisdom check-in partner: mentor. wisdom is not common. Wisdom is not obvious. Wisdom is indeed rare. Wisdom is not hereditary. Wisdom is earned and learned. Wisdom is based on observation. And diligence. Perseverance. Wisdom requires not fainting. Wisdom does not take breaks. Wisdom does have brakes though. Wisdom knows when to speak and when to be silent. Wisdom has discretion. Wisdom does not shame others. Wisdom does not wane or tarry. Wisdom needs to share wisdom. As a wise woman, this is essential to support the Crown.

As a woman, we see Crowns as important and regal. Crowns are misunderstood, though. Real Crowns are heavy. Crowns require work. Crowns speak to the public that you are responsible and respectful. Crowns are earned. Crowns create a spotlight. This spotlight that it casts is unique. With this light, responsibility. There is a statement which says 'heavy is the head that wears the Crown.'

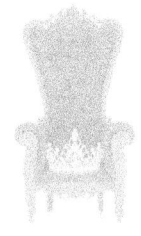

Wisdom for the Crown concerns itself with image. The image has to be protected. There are some rules that apply to Crowns that you are subject to. The rules of the Crown are hypocritical. The rules are imposed on the Crown but these rules are different from all others for all others.

Observe and listen.

Keep the Crown wise.

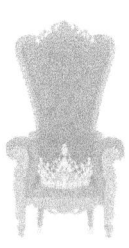

The Crown Has Worth

> [10] A wife of noble character who can find?
> She is worth far more than rubies.
> [11] Her husband has full confidence in her
> and lacks nothing of value.
> [12] She brings him good, not harm,
> all the days of her life.
> [13] She selects wool and flax
> and works with eager hands.
> [14] She is like the merchant ships,
> bringing her food from afar.
>
> Proverbs 31:10–14

A wife?! Whew! The idea of being a wife is interesting and highly coveted. The role of a wife is the goal of most women. Most women try to make that happen in college an some even in high school. Some get it but then are forced to divorce. Others don't ever get that prize.

The role of wife is a prize, or at least it is supposed to be. The Crown is coupled with being a wife. The Crown and the wife have worth. The Crown and the wife are not synonymous. You can have worth and a Crown without being a wife. So, the worth of the Crown is based on who you are as a woman.

The wife needs to study her role in order to be effective at the role. As a wife, you have a role and responsibilities. If you don't have good intentions, then graciously bow out of the opportunity. The role of life is the matriarch of the family, which means that you are the female leader of the family. You control the culture and climate of the family. You control the temperature of the home and the family. The Crown has worth whether you are a wife or not.

The husband has complete confidence in her, the wife. He has that confidence because she has done a good job. When you consider the characteristics of a great wife, they are aligned with being a great woman. You have to be a great woman in order to be a great wife. Being a wife is extra - you are a woman first.

Love. Joy. Peace. Gentleness. Patience. Faithful. Goodness. Kindness. Loving. Lovable. Thinker. Researcher. Charitable. Honest. Healthy. Nurturer. Reader. Warm. Friendly. Compassionate. Passionate. Innovator. Self-control. Helpful. Creative. Welcoming. Spiritual.

These characteristics are subjective however, think of all of the women that you admire, either up close or at a distance. Those women all have some of these traits. This is not a wish list and everything on this list is within your reach and is part of your skill set. The woman who exhibits and embodies these characteristics are women who should be successful but are definitely successful women.

What does being a wife mean to you? Where does that definition originate? Wife has changed since 1900. Since 1950. Since 2000. since 2020. It will change again and again. It also changes

between people. The role and definition of a wife is based on the wife's perception of the role, the husband, then her family background impacts as well as societal standards. Now, the wife has to consider how to proceed as a woman and wife, help mate and nurturer. This role is not an easy one but it is an important one.

Her husband offers her worth. His valuation offers her extra value. She is uplifted by his words and his deeds.

The role of a helpmate - wife is to help her husband. They are supposed to help each other with the goals and family activities. The marriage unit is a cohesive unit that moves together and compliments each other, and keeping focus on the family business so that the entire family can prosper.

The woman who was an entrepreneur helps the Crown have worth. The entrepreneur offers her flexibility and her family so that she is available for the requirements of the husband and children and other family members.

Verse 13 reads: 'and [she] works with eager hands.' This speaks to your work ethic as a woman. The power of your worthy ethic is far reaching. The work ethic is something that you share with others through observation and direct teaching. Work ethic is shared with others so that they too can have work ethic - something most people need but don't have. Your kids need your work ethic, so that your work ethic needs to be top-notch. With eager hands is the opposite of lazy. It is definitely the opposite of 'I don't feel like it.' It is definitely the process of understanding what it means to work and produce results.

Verse 14 reads, 'she is like merchant ships, bringing her food from afar.' In the same spirit of entrepreneurship, you need to ensure that you explore your gifts. After you discover your gifts, then you are to use your gifts to help others to move forward. If you are not currently doing that, you should decide soon to make a different decision. When you don't use your gifts, then you are being selfish. You have been blessed because others were operating in their God-given gifts. What will you do if the people who were supposed to teach and mentor you opted out or quit? Where would you go? Who is the backup for that absence? So, don't do that. Use your gifts as you have been ordered.

The Crown has worth. As you consider your personal sense of worth, what do you see and feel? What do you notice? What do you wonder? Is it your worth that fuels your daily achievements and accomplishments? Or is it your lack of worth that causes you to keep trying to reach the remotest dreams that you have?

The Crown has work. Worth is defined as value associated with benefits. The work is what forces respect and sometimes creates a following. So that others can be inspired to follow their own goals and share their gifts.

Marrianne Williamson wrote some words that knits this together.

"Our deepest fear is not that we are inadequate. Our deepest fear is that we are powerful beyond measure. It is our light, not our darkness that most frightens us. We ask ourselves, 'Who am I to be brilliant, gorgeous, talented, fabulous?' Actually, who are you not to be? You are a child of God. Your playing small does not serve the world. There is nothing enlightened about shrinking so that other people won't feel insecure around you. We are all

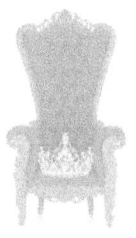

meant to shine, as children do. We were born to make manifest the glory of God that is within us. It's not just in some of us; it's in everyone. And as we let our own light shine, we unconsciously give other people permission to do the same. As we are liberated from our own fear, our presence automatically liberates others."

Williamson put these words together and this will inspire you to take a proverbial leap toward understanding and owning your worth.

The Crown has worth but you should not need to be convinced of this worth. You are in need of a self-esteem revival. There needs to be a reunion with you and yourself esteem. The average woman cannot look at herself in the mirror without shame and criticism. NOTHING is wrong with YOU. You are already WHOLE. You are already IT. You are already ENOUGH.

The Crown has worth. That worth is not dependent on ANYTHING. You doubted your worth because you feel that you need to be someone else's definition of perfect. That is not how the Crown's worth is determined. God established your worth in Genesis 1: 27 when He stated that He made you in His likeness and image. The modifications that we have made are not His fault. You made changes to you based on societal influences, in response to some man that you hoped understood your worth but he never did, and the people who were afraid to understand you because you changed every game, in every setting that you are a part of. That is my story and yours may be similar, but at least be willing to tell the truth - at least to yourself. You tried to fit in and you are still failing at that. Because the Crown has worth, you cannot fit into most settings.

The Crown has worth. Without the need for modifications of the default settings. What if you grew up in a 'bubble' where you were not exposed to the various events, people, and other outside influences, and inside influences that have crippled and/or dismantle your self-esteem. If your self-esteem were intact at the enhanced default setting status, then you would be holding your Crown at the worth height. You would know that the Crown has worth. You would behave like the Crown has worth.

The Crown has unbelievable worth.

THE CROWN WORKS

¹⁵ She gets up while it is still night;
she provides food for her family
and portions for her female servants.
¹⁶ She considers a field and buys it;
out of her earnings she plants a vineyard.
¹⁷ She sets about her work vigorously;
her arms are strong for her tasks.
¹⁸ She sees that her trading is profitable,
and her lamp does not go out at night.
¹⁹ In her hand she holds the distaff
and grasps the spindle with her fingers.
²⁰ She opens her arms to the poor
and extends her hands to the needy.

Proverbs 31:15–20

The Crown has worth.

The Crown works.

Some kind of fabulous woman. Kind of like you? Yes, kind of like you. She has a business - an entrepreneur. She followed her calling and her dreams.

15

She gets up while it is still night;

   she provides food for her family

and portions for her female servants.

We, of course, do not know what time that the woman in these verses gets into bed for the evening, but we know that she does not have a phone, Facebook, Instagram, or Tik Tok. So, a disciplined woman has time considerations, such as children in bed by 8:00 p.m., no later than 8:30 p.m. She is taking care of her household needs and now it is husband time. You need to talk and connect with him before you fall asleep.

Now, all of that because you get up at dark. Before everyone. Remember, you were the last went to sleep. And the first one awake and working. Breakfast is made when they all wake up and have prepared for the day. Yes, you do have some help. I don't know where she gets all these female servants from but they are to do the chores that she delegates to them.

The Crown works.

In order for the Crown to work, she has to have a plan and the desire to make it happen. Most of us have a dream/plan but we sometimes fail to execute. We don't have enough fuel to execute the plans/dreams that have been planted inside of us.

So, when the Crown works, please consider the work that the Crown will do. Is the work good? Does it help others? Does it fund your life? Will you need an additional source of income? Will this work keep you away from your family for difficult, extended periods of time? Will you be able to travel with your family when you are out of school? Will your work cause harm to your image and family's safety? Will it compromise your

values? Will it last for the lifetime of your family? Can it be passed on for generations to come?

What will the Crown do?

She provides food for her family. This does not mean that she cooks daily but she does not use delivery service daily either. Balance.

16

She considers a field and buys it;

> out of her earnings she plants a vineyard.

Entrepreneurship is the work. Real estate is her preference. Make your own choice. But this is critical for your work and your well-being.

17

She sets about her work vigorously;

> her arms are strong for her tasks.

Vigorously is the opposite of lazy and procrastination. Her arms exercise and she is fit. We have work to do. Are you lazy? Are you committed? Are you consistent? Are you focused? Are you creative? Are you a researcher? Are you innovative? Do you have perseverance? Do you have willpower?

The strong arms are both literal and metaphorical. She actually is fit. She takes care of her heart and her body. She actually stays fit because for daily activity and her focus on self-care. We should do the same. What do you do to take care of your health? wellness? Self-care? Weight management? Do you drink the right amount of water? Do you get the right amount of sleep? Do you eat properly, the correct proteins, vegetables, and grains? Do you have annual medical check-ups? Do you take vitamins? These questions will lead you to the path that you should travel so that you can be proud of your appearance and feelings. You are in charge of this aspect of your life. Master that time and moment while you have control over that process.

Work to stop the excuses that we so easily develop when these topics surface. You recall that you have said that you wish that you could do something but when you have the opportunity, do you miss it? Please use all of your time/days wisely. None are promised. We experienced a pandemic in 2020 which lasted for a couple of years. This pandemic was caused by Covid-19. This disease caused the death of over 1 million people, most of which never were buried properly. Time is not your friend. Time is not on your side. Time is not guaranteed. Stop treating it as if it is.

18

She sees that her trading is profitable,

    and her lamp does not go out at night.

Based on that scripture, she is profitable in her business dealings. Her business is healthy and profitable. She tends to it with the utmost care.

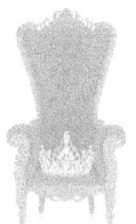

While we have explored the hard work that she exhibits, it bears repeating that she does not have idle time. The lesson here for the modern woman is that we need to be wiser with our time.

The lamp does not go out at night because she is working hard and studying her craft. The time that she spends on her business and family matters is how she is successful. She is probably not playing games on her phone or scrolling Facebook, Instagram, or Tik Tok. She is not taking selfies and gossiping. What of her example do you need to leave it to your life and lifestyle?

What do you need to change in order to make sure that you're taking care of your family and your responsibilities? When I was getting my second and third degrees, both masters, I stopped watching television. I could only watch three hours of television each week because I am writing two papers each week and reading hundreds of pages. I was also raising two small children. I was working a full-time job and was running a publishing company. I was trying to make a marriage work. I could not afford to spend my time frivolously. I had to be hyperfocused. I needed to have outrageous discipline.

19

In her hand she holds the distaff

    and grasps the spindle with her fingers.

This is the evidence of the work that she does and that she is focused on.

20

She opens her arms to the poor

    and extends her hands to the needy.

She is a charity-centered person as well. She donates to organizations who help those in need. She volunteers her time to those who are in need. She considers charity important and she does not gloat or brag about her work or her contributions.

The Crown works for the benefit and consideration of the family. The Crown works because you have talent and obligations.

The Crown is successful.

The Crown works.

THE CROWN IS

> [21] When it snows, she has no fear for her household;
> for all of them are clothed in scarlet.
> [22] She makes coverings for her bed;
> she is clothed in fine linen and purple.
> [23] Her husband is respected at the city gate,
> where he takes his seat among the elders of the land.
> [24] She makes linen garments and sells them,
> and supplies the merchants with sashes.
> [25] She is clothed with strength and dignity;
> she can laugh at the days to come.
> [26] She speaks with wisdom,
> and faithful instruction is on her tongue.
>
> Proverbs 31:21–26

21

When it snows, she has no fear for her household;

for all of them are clothed in scarlet.

Being clothed in scarlet is a protection mechanism. Scarlet is a type of very fine and high-quality wool cloth which as such preserves warmth. And when colored, also appears dignified and rich. This sounds like a red wool coat. Women look great in red wool coats. Can you imagine a family portrait in a red wool coat? That would be an amazing portrait.

But they are not cold either because she's prepared for winter. Prepared and fashionable is what we need to take note of.

She is industrious and innovative. These coverings for her beds and the other things she makes further confirms that she is creative and crafty. She is a planner; a logistics Queen.

22

She makes coverings for her bed;

    she is clothed in fine linen and purple.

Her image is important, so she dresses in the finest clothing. Linen and other natural materials such as silk or fine materials that offer the best opportunity to show class and refinement. She manages her hair, nails, feet, eyebrows, and waxing/shaving as needed.

Purple is a regal and royal color. Purple brings out the best in you. Purple brings compliments and offers you a safe place to retreat. Purple is a royal color which requires different and more refined behavior. Purple changes your life and perspective.

23

Her husband is respected at the city gate,

    where he takes his seat among the elders of the land.

Her husband is an upstanding person; this comes with mate selection. Many women have this problem: we pick the wrong guy. We pick the guy that we thought picked us but we should have picked a man who we have selected. As of 2023, women

outnumber men 7 to 1. Men believe that they have the upper hand so they make the selection process competitive and complicated, overwhelming and heart breaking.

Many men have been dating multiple women in order to have a choice while they make them feel like they're the only one. Some men have been in more than one relationship, requiring him to stop seeing a woman on Thursday because he is marrying another woman on Saturday. Imagine the shock and pain. Women are seen as nosy if they do a background check or hire a private investigator so that this won't happen. Men are not being honest. The issues are monstrous. The women are not quite desperate but are certainly vulnerable about the desire to be in a relationship, a meaningful one, so that they can spend the rest of their lives with someone that they can believe loves her, respects her, and does not cheat on her.

A woman needs an honorable man. A woman needs to be honorable. The couple needs to be honorable together. The elders at the gate, the wise people that you know, will help you understand your life. Invest in those relationships.

24

She makes linen garments and sells them,

    and supplies the merchants with sashes.

She is a creator and a wholesaler. She makes her own garments and sells them. She had already earned the title of entrepreneur. She further expanded the scope of her business. Her gift of logistics is the key to her success but both at home and in her business. She is into the details. She respects the work that she

has chosen. She is good at her profession. She is attentive to her customers.

25

She is clothed with strength and dignity;

    she can laugh at the days to come.

Respect. Strength. Dignity. She wears those attributes. How does one wear these details? Behavior. Actions. Words. Places she visits. Goals that she sets. She respects herself so she behaves in a manner that others respect her as well.

As women, we need to consider carefully the story that we let others tell on our behalf. We control that by address, our attitude, our behavior, and our speech. We have to go we have to guard our image carefully because it is very hard to recover a harmed reputation. Because of this, we need to put a heavy guard around our reputation. Years are needed to build a great reputation and only minutes in order to change that reputation.

Take full control of your image and reputation. Consider how you impact the image of others when you do not protect your own image and reputation.

No bonnets. No house slippers. No short shorts. Nothing that causes reproach for the family. Your word and your reputation is who you are!

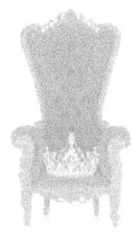

26

She speaks with wisdom,

   and faithful instruction is on her tongue.

She does not gossip. She does not spread rumors. She does not speak to people in a mean manner. She does not tear people apart with her words. She does not hurt people with her words. She does not use your words against you. She is forgiving when she is harmed. She is faithful to her family, friends, work, and her philosophy. She is kind. She is loving. She is compassionate. She is empathetic. She is patient. She is invested. She is an optimist. She continues to look for the silver lining and all things. She believes in the good in people. She is not a doubter. She is respected. She is admired. She is encouraged. She is encouraging. She is well-meaning. She is a critical thinker.

All of these qualities contribute to her wisdom and her ability to offer faithful instruction. She guards her tongue and uses to uplift others and assist in helping their self-esteem. She's a beacon of hope and light.

The Crown is.

She is all of this and more.

She is the Crown.

She has to function in the manner that the Crown does. She is you.

You have to respond in the same manner as the Crown. You need to respond with the respect as the Crown. You are.

Spiritual Messages for Women

The Crown is.

THE CROWN'S WORK

> [27] She watches over the affairs of her household
> and does not eat the bread of idleness.
> [28] Her children arise and call her blessed;
> her husband also, and he praises her:
> [29] "Many women do noble things,
> but you surpass them all."
> [30] Charm is deceptive, and beauty is fleeting;
> but a woman who fears the Lord is to be praised.
> [31] Honor her for all that her hands have done,
> and let her works bring her praise at the city gate.
>
> Proverbs 31:27–31

A few chapters ago we discussed the "Crown Works," so this is the Crown's Work. As a woman, we have one job: our children and our husbands; our households.

As we watch over our households, we research the best methods for all aspects. We research the best homes, best neighborhoods, best schools, best child care, best transportation, best businesses, best deals for purchases, best colleges, best investments, best food, best toys, and anything else we need for our families. We do not have time to be idle and do nothing. We, women, work harder in this capacity than men.

When your family praises you, what have you done? Achieved? What have you done to earn that praise? Did you do everything perfectly? Did you get everything correct correctly? Did you make them happy? Did you give them everything that they asked

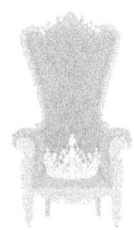

for? Did you let it cause harm without penalty? Did you let them have a meal full of snacks and without vegetables? Did you let them miss their homework or miss school? Did you decide against establishing a curfew? Did you let them get themselves well when they were sick? Did you let them steal candy from the store? Did you let them watch inappropriate television shows or movies? Did you forget to pick up the supplies for the school project? Did you neglect the haircuts? Did you forget to teach them to bathe themselves or to clean their rooms? Do you let them leave their toys all over the house? Did you neglect to teach them to cook? Did you neglect to teach them to wash their own clothes? Did you fail to teach them about paying bills and credit? There are at least 1,000 more questions like this and the answer to most of them will be no.

Because these answers will be no, then you are due that praise and honor. You deserve this honor and this praise. This is the light that they bestow upon you motivates you to keep going, to keep being wife and mom, to keep being great, to keep being a major contributor to society, and to keep focused on the world for which you are responsible. Keep doing it well - what you do. EVERYDAY! Keep the written praise so that you that when you feel down, then you're able to look at those notes and remember how you felt when you read it the first time. These words are powerful at your greatest need.

Your husband and children should praise you and honor you. You should be a woman worthy of praise.

But you surpass them all is quite the compliment. The nobility is sometimes not about what you do, it is more about who you are. This is a strong statement and compliment.

30

Charm is deceptive, and beauty is fleeting;

    but a woman who fears the Lord is to be praised.

Most women have been charming their whole lives. Charm means the art of persuasion. The art of persuasion had been interested and invested is the extension of charming. Charm is deceitful in some very famous instances. Charm should not replace truth or be a distraction from your life's reality. Charm is attractive to the surface but has no value in an authentic relationship. Charm is temporary. Charm is not steadfast or reliable.

Beauty is valued over all else by society. The advertisements and commercial businesses honor the beauty. The beautiful people are always honored more than those who are labeled as less than beautiful. Beautiful is always what is treasured, but is that what defines a woman? What happens to a beautiful woman when she is older? Her beauty may actually fade but what is most important is who she is on the inside.

Are you beautiful on the inside? Who are you on the inside? Are you a beautiful person? What kind of person are you? What happens on the inside should be seen and experienced on the outside with others. We are all working to be better, to be graceful, to be pleasant, to be well received, to be more liked, and to be well respected.

Because of your insides, you fear the Lord. That woman is to be praised. Most people misunderstand what fear of the Lord means. Fearing the Lord means that you regard the Lord and His commandments, you share your life with others as needed, and you give to others the way that God says to do so.

Praise sometimes is confusing and misleading. Praise is not because you are better than the next woman. Praise is because you are a woman who God has gifted and called and you have done well in God's sight.

This life is hard at most points, but as a woman considers her life, both past and future, her work represents her worth. She will be remembered for all of the work she has done and all that she will do. All of the people that she touched and all those that she reached will be the voices and votes when her honor is due to her. This will also be the tickets for her praise. Your life's grade and impact are the sun of your love, your work, your contribution, your volunteerism, your words, and your goals. Your achievements and your desires are part of that grade and impact.

Your work is your Crown.

The Crown's Work.

His GPS for the Crown

With a Map, a Flashlight, and a Snack

> [22] He who finds a wife finds what is good
> and receives favor from the Lord.
>
> Proverbs 18:22

GPS, global positioning system, give directions to the locations of your choice. You enter an address, then it speaks the turn-by-turn directions to your destination. GPS arrived in the United States in 1973 and was in full public use in 1995. Up to 1995, we used paper maps.

AAA issued trip ticks to their members when they requested a map of a road trip. The team would outline the route in orange highlighter. I was always intrigued with that orange highlighter. On all of our trips as a family, I always wondered where the page was going to be highlighted in orange.

These maps have taken families to all parts of the country. Maps of also have been housed in a binder that real estate agents use called a key map. Then there's an atlas. These tools are designed to get you to your destination. The reason paper maps are no longer popular or well used is because the construction is so extensive that the maps are often out of date upon publication.

So, GPS became popular and widely used because of the construction and the out-of-date maps.

God's GPS is not like those other tools. God's GPS is never out of date or behind construction or is never offline. God's GPS is never taking you in the wrong direction. It may feel as though it is but it is not. God knows what He is doing. There have been days that I have doubted His directions and plans, but I cannot doubt and follow. You have to pick one. You cannot have both.

God's direction for the Crown is never going to be tailored to your eyes and ears. God puts you where He needs you to be; not where you want to be. Your desires may come to His attention but He needs your gifts, talents, and personality on particular places at a particular time.

Have you wondered what God is doing? Have you ever tried to get a new job and you were declined everywhere? Or there was a high or difficult hurdle in your past? Do you feel forced to stay in a place that you don't like or don't feel that you fit in? But because He needs you there, He has blocked your path out of the location. Have you ever felt that way? I have definitely felt that way. But I soon realized that until I have accomplished the mission at that location, I won't be able to leave. This is a time that we consider how to achieve the mission expeditiously if we want to leave that job.

The flashlight is designed to shine the light directly on the situation. The light provides clarity. The light will provide clarity while on the path. The light drives away evil and darkness. The light ensures that you do not get lost. The light creates warmth and comfort. The light welcomes.

The snack curbs hunger and it ensures that you are not distracted by the side shows and the dramatics. The snack gives you endurance -- we cannot afford to quit too soon. The snack makes sure to be stay the course and stay on course. We need the sustenance to ensure that we have the needed staying power. We need that snack so that we can settle the hunger then go right back to the path that the GPS has outlined for us.

God's GPS for the Crown can be simple some days but be rugged and complicated on other days. None of the path will be revealed until it is time to travel these paths. The people on the journey are also important. They are specifically designed to be there in order to bless you and some of which you will bless.

God's GPS will never lead anywhere without a purpose and without a mission.

He that findeth a wife, finds a good thing. How will he find you? This is a tricky location. This requires paying attention and being emotionally available. Are you available when he does show up? Are you going to recognize him? Will you know that God sent you to him and vice versa?

God's GPS is not broken. He knows what He is doing. You need to have more belief and faith. This is a marathon, not a sprint.

Keep your Crown steady and level, focused and forgiving.

God's GPS for the Crown.

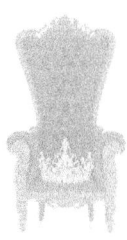

The Crown Has Standards

What Time is Your Flight?

³² Then you will know the truth, and the truth will set you free."

John 8:32

Freedom has many definitions. Freedom has many connotations. Emotional freedom is the best freedom. The best freedom is the peace that comes when you tell the truth - especially to yourself.

The first person that you want to start telling the truth to is yourself. You have lied to yourself on more than one occasion, on a regular basis. You have lied to yourself for good reasons and bad reasons and for no reason. You've sacrificed yourself in many ways. You have a lied to yourself for other people to be okay.

Why do you lie to yourself? Why do you continue to lie to yourself? Why don't you take a stand for yourself? The thoughts in your head and your heart need to be focused on what is truthful. The problem with the truth is that it may hurt and it may not be palatable. It may be confusing and it may be distancing you from others.

Lying to make yourself feel better is not the best policy for a healthy well-being. What happens that we lie to ourselves? What does it mean when we lie to ourselves? What can we do to stop lying to ourselves?

When will you change your pattern of lying to yourself? What does that require?

This means that you need to stop making deals and negotiating with yourself. In these situations, we are clearly trying to stop something from happening so we make a deal with ourselves so that we can make a worse deal with someone else.

When is your flight? When do you start with the truth?

The truth about:

Who you are.

What you want out of life.

What you need to be a whole woman.

Who you are not.

What do you not want out of life.

What you have neglected about your life.

What have you overlooked for yourself.

What you wish you had but you don't.

What you wish that you had but never will.

What lies you have told.

What secrets you are keeping.

What you are hiding.

What you are trying to escape.

What you have missed in life.

What you know.

What you don't know.

What you need to know.

Who has harmed you.

Whom you have harmed.

Things which have harmed you.

Things which have damaged you.

Things which you have done to harm others.

Things which you have done to damage others.

What you need to look at yourself in the mirror without being critical.

What you need to be a whole woman.

What you need to be a great woman.

What you need to be the woman that you can be proud of.

Who you will become.

What you contribute to this world.

Who can help.

What you believe.

What you don't believe.

What is important to you.

What you will fight for.

Who you will fight for.

What you won't fight for.

What will you not speak up for.

What do you not allow yourself to consider.

Some of these questions will require a lifetime to find answers to. We must make the necessary changes daily in order to become a better woman.

Set yourself free.

What time is your flight? Your flight to freedom? The flight which no lies are necessary to be whole and complete.

Stop calculating the cost of your freedom based on what will happen to someone else as a result.

THE CROWN DECIDES PRIORITIES

³⁸ As Jesus and his disciples were on their way, he came to a village where a woman named Martha opened her home to him. ³⁹ She had a sister called Mary, who sat at the Lord's feet listening to what he said. ⁴⁰ But Martha was distracted by all the preparations that had to be made. She came to him and asked, "Lord, don't you care that my sister has left me to do the work by myself? Tell her to help me!"

⁴¹ "Martha, Martha," the Lord answered, "you are worried and upset about many things,

Luke 10:38–41

Life has so many decisions to be made. We have so many decisions to make to live, to grow, to eat, to love, to educate, to be fierce, to be kind, to be compassionate, to be a leader, to be a survivor, to pray, to forgive, to believe, to serve, to be extraordinary, to be dynamic, and to be fabulous.

We all know Mary's and Martha's; sometimes we are the Mary's and other times, the Martha's. What does it take to make the right decision? What is required to have the correct priorities? What happens when your priorities are misplaced? How does this happen -- your priorities are not in the right place? Jesus is days away from being executed so He is at Mary's house teaching. While Mary's listening, Martha is working.

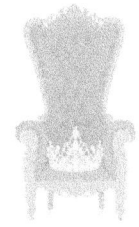

Mary is listening to Jesus. Martha is working for Jesus. They are both doing what they feel is important and they disagree about these current activities.

Why do they disagree? They both have a point to make regarding their decisions. Mary was fine with saying nothing to Martha about her activity but Martha was not okay with Mary's activity. Martha finally asked Jesus to make Mary help her with the work that she chose. Martha fully expected Jesus to take her side, however Jesus told Martha that she was wrong. Jesus told Martha that she could not count on any help from Mary and that she had made the wrong choice. Martha was devastated. She could not imagine how this could possibly be the case. How could Mary be doing the right thing and not her?

Jesus taught Mary that while she was not wrong, Mary was more correct. Timing was essential in this lesson. Jesus was here on Earth for limited time. Jesus was teaching. Jesus was sharing. Jesus was living. Jesus was doing what He would not be ever doing again. Jesus was teaching Martha that the choice to spend time with Him was more important than the work she was doing. She could have done that work later. Martha needs to be able to see this for herself. She takes time for granted even though she is meticulous about her duties. She needs to learn to assess the situation and hand in order to determine whether the dishes can wait when spending time with an important person, such as Jesus. This happens to us. Sometimes we get our timing wrong. We don't always make the best decisions for timing. We miss significant opportunities for frivolous stuff. Like Martha, we need to have to adjust our judgment of our view of our presence surroundings. Like Martha, we have been in this rut/routine for most of our lives and we fail to recognize the importance of the present.

Mary had chosen to sit at the feet of Jesus and listen to whatever Jesus was saying and teaching. Mary had decided that she needed to hear what Jesus had to say because she seem to know that his time would be sure that she needed to use this time this way. She had chosen the better way to spend her time -- in the presence of Jesus. She understood the importance of this time and his messages.

Mary made the decision that we need to make: the most important one. We often have chances to make decisions but we don't use the right decision-making tree. Some decisions require decision flowchart or matrix or tree because the decisions are complex and intense; the lifetime outcome has long-term effects. Important decisions need detailed thoughts and a decision chart. There are other decisions that don't have time for decision charges; they are time sensitive ones and emergency ones.

Decisions like home buying requires detailed thought. Fixing your time requires immediate attention. Spending time with Jesus versus cleaning the house versus preparing food for guests are not comparable to each other.

People make decisions based on different factors. We need to make sure that the decisions that we make are ones that we can be proud of and are ones which make the most impact on our lives and the world. Mary made the better decision. Martha thought that she was a more responsible person. Our priorities are important and they need to be aligned with a life that we are responsible for. Priorities are important. Making the right decisions at the right time so that the wrong decisions don't cost you the life or finances that you have eagerly worked so hard for.

Be the woman who considers the priorities so that the biggest impact on the world, so that you learn the most, so that you will love better, so that you will think better, and so you will reaffirm your commitment to your life's work.

Parties all your responsibility as a woman with a Crown. Handle them well.

The Crown Rests

> ²⁸ "Come to me, all you who are weary and heavy-laden, and I will give you rest.
>
> Matthew 11:28

Most women forget to rest. Most women do not ask God for rest. We want it all. We want it now. We are in a hurry to have it. We are moving at an unbelievable pace. Because of that pace, we are EXHAUSTED. We are also OVERWHELMED. We are tired, but we won't admit it. We won't admit it because we are too proud. We are too busy to admit it because we have too much to do.

The Crown has responsibilities and that to-do list is so long! Everybody that you care for has needs. You want to take care of each one of them and each one of their needs.

The first lesson in rest is to get some help. Help is getting and ordering service, such as having groceries and household items delivered and shipped to you. There should be a mental release that it is okay to delegate such items out. We want it all but we don't have to do it all. We as women hold ourselves to a standard that says we don't ask for help and we don't delegate and we don't depend on anyone. That is not a good or reliable standard. this is quite the change in how things are done. Women never depend on other women and we have been taught to never let them see you sweat or cry. that is terrible advice! We need to be comfortable being our truest selves -- whoever that is.

Help. Get services to help you with your tasks. There's no shame in that.

Now, I do not suggest you get people to sit at games to your children's games because that is your job and that is because mothering is a non-delegatable job, but everything else is something that you can delegate.

Help is an assistant if you have a business or want to start one. Help is using audible books or the freelancer service app. Help is collaborating with friends about what they are doing to solve similar problems. Help is getting professionals to help you with travel, cleaning, car repairs, and home repairs.

Help is a cleaning service for your home. This is a contentious point for women. There are women who believe that a cleaning lady is needed and necessary; they would not live without one. They know the value and the opportunity cost of personally doing the cleaning versus visiting the museum in those same two to three hours for the money that it cost you, which is less than the purse or that concert ticket. In some areas, housekeeping services are $150 for a cleaning that takes two to three hours. Two to three people clean your home. It would have taken you several hours to do that same job; not to mention that you would have gotten sidetracked several times during the cleaning process.

There are women who feel that having a cleaning team is an insult to their womanhood if they don't clean their own homes. These are normally traditionally reared women who were

disturbed in their sleep as a child early on Saturday mornings in order to clean alongside their mother. These women may want to have help with their home cleaning but they will never let their mother or matriarchs know because they are embarrassed or they will embarrass their mother. If you as a woman cannot imagine doing this, then don't but don't feel pressured to do so because others do so.

Housekeeping is your choice because of the stigma that our families place on the value of the clean home that was done personally. It is your choice but please consider the tradeoff of getting a housekeeper so that you can spend quality time with your spouse and your children. Forgive yourself. Let someone clean your house. Help.

The Crown should have help. In biblical days, these women had maid servants, but we feel less than a woman. What happened in the transition? How did this happen? Executives have assistants, so you should as well.

Effective Crowns have help. They also accept this help well. They delegate with poise and grace. We cannot do all that we'll call and gifted to do without help.

Without help, there is stress, imminent stress, so also there is a therapist when you are not able to talk to others about your mental and emotional wellness. In some communities, there's a stigma for counseling, so we don't usually go see a counselor, but we may need to do so for our mental and emotional well-being. Don't be afraid. Don't be concerned about what others will say to you about taking care of yourself. Most of us are

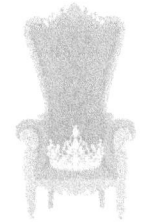

afraid to seek this help because we are afraid of who we are and what we will find out about ourselves.

Help is the hair stylist, the nail technician, the pedicure lady, the esthetician, the masseuse, and the shoe salesperson. Don't forget to share ride driver. These are all people who help you to relax, prioritize, and be your best self.

Help. Self-care includes the aforementioned spa services as well as taking the time for yourself because the Crown needs to refuel and refresh, relax and rejuvenate, reflect and revive the woman that you are. When you are tired, then you need to stop and assess your life for where you need help. Then get it.

Stop ignoring your need for help. Be responsible. This scripture is one of my favorites. The Lord will give you rest. Ask. Seek. Request. Then relax so you can accept it.

The rest is essential to you not having a meltdown, being ineffective, and being overwhelmed. powerful, effective, and respected Crowns know when to relax, rest, release, and rejuvenate. This pace of life is rigorous. Rest is required.

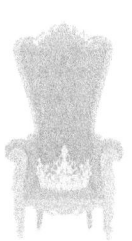

THE CROWN'S EXTRAVAGANCE

¹³ love extravagantly.

1 Corinthians 13:13b MSG

Love. Extravagantly. Love extravagantly. This is beyond the boundaries that most people have. Extravagantly is the only way to love. The definition of extravagance is unrestrained or fantastic access; recklessness, outrageousness. Love in the most ridiculous of measures. Love that doesn't make any sense.

Extravagance is also associated with wastefulness. Too much food. Too many clothes. Too much wine. Too much of anything is a waste. But not love. No one can ever have too much love.

This version of the verse stands out because it ensures that love is not optional. It states that love is valuable and extremely important. Most people have never experienced authentic love. Most people have only seen conditional love and action. Anyone can love with conditions and stipulations, based on some special circumstances. If your relationship has any conditions or strings attached then that relationship is not love. There is not a label for that but it is definitely not love.

Love is a verb. Love is known by what you do, and only if it matches what you say. So, by definition of love extravagantly,

do it big! Love is not only paying the bills, it is hugs and conversations, dates and reading together. Love includes some nots: no physical, mental, or emotional abuse; no disrespect, no ignoring, no drama, no cheating, and no disappearing acts. The list could go on but you get the idea.

Love extravagantly means that you go above and beyond. Love with all of yourself. Love with more than what you thought you were capable of. Love at the beyond reasonable manner. Love matters. Love makes a difference in every person's life. When you see people who are hurting in a very deep place, please consider the source or lack thereof the love of their life. Many failed issues can be traced back to how much love you have experienced. It is the same for all of us. You deserve love. You have always deserved love. From the time of your birth until today, you still deserve love.

Hurt will stall you from being able to love. Harm will keep you from loving others freely, authentically. The one thing that you need to be concerned about is being able to love after you have been hurt or harmed. If you cannot love, then you need to seek some help to heal from what wounded you. Counseling to whole is about self-love. That is the first and most important love.

There is a scripture that reads love one another. There's a verse about brotherly love - agape. Because of this scripture, there was a billboard created which reads: 'When I said love one another, I meant that.' - God.

The reason we cannot love one another is because we don't love ourselves. If you can't love yourself, then loving someone else is

a high marker. It is very hard, if not impossible to do so, to love another person.

Loving extravagantly requires all of your focus and all of your power, all of your energy and all of your chemistry, all of your mind and all of your heart, all of your fierceness and all of your might. Loving extravagantly requires your inner being and your mental prowess. Loving extravagantly depends on your capacity for mental, emotional, and physical commitment. Lack of love started with an internal struggle. Loving extravagantly is the only option when you are all in.

Poker has a phrase that is the most intense phrase ever: I'm all in. 'I'm all in' is said when the player has faith in their cards, so much so that the player pushes ALL of their chips into the center of the table as they announce those words.

Those words are the expression of the extravagance of love. ALL in! Nothing can move you from this place of love if you are all in. Freedom exists in extravagant love! You can be your truest self when you love without boundaries or caution, without limits or fear. Find out who you are when you love and give that love all that you have. Your 100% without regret.

Love extravagantly.

Be all in.

For yourself.

For those you love.

Love is a verb. Love is what we do.

THE CROWN HAS WRATH

KEEP YOUR WITS ABOUT YOU

> [26] "In your anger do not sin": Do not let the sun go down while you are still angry, [27] and do not give the devil a foothold.
>
> Ephesians 4:26–27

There will be some tough times. Some days won't be pleasant. We as women will be judged by how we respond to the trauma and the issues that we endure and survive.

We are not all entrepreneurs; some of us have careers so we have bosses. Our careers are frustrating. We have traffic issues. We have family issues. We have some conflict at home. We have crises. We have dark times. We have enemies. We have flaws and faults. We make mistakes. We get angry. We can angry with ourselves. We get angry with others.

In this verse, it acknowledges that you will have anger. Anger is inevitable. It then implores you to avoid sin while and when angry. Quite the task admittedly.

Do not sin while you are angry. Do not do something that you will regret and you cannot recover from. Don't ruin relationships that you will want later. Don't make decisions that you will later

regret and that will cost you more severely than you can afford. Don't say words that will render irreparable damage; the words that make you wish that you could change some things about how you address the matter in its entirety even if you work for it.

In your anger, do not sin.

Is revenge really worth it? Do you really want to do that? Will you want that done to you?

As a woman, learn to regulate your temperament. Your response and reaction are a deal maker for you. Those two elements are respect gatherers. You are a Crown. You are the jewel. This cannot be consumed with poor decisions and wrath. This makes for a poorly received Crown. The Crown has wrath but cannot continue on that path. You cannot be continuously angry because that will consume you. You have work to do. This work cannot be sidetracked by the wrath that exists.

In your anger, do not sin.

Do not let the sun set on your wrath. Easy translation: do not go to bed angry. Do not let this wrath fester so long that it takes over your inner being. Do not live in the area of the anger and in the presence of the anger. The anger cannot live. You cannot give it life.

Constant anger, either consistent or repetitive, is not healthy. Rather than anger or used interchangeably however for this text,

they will be used separately. Anger is what happens first. Wrath happens next. Wrath is caused by anger. It is the consequence to the person who has made you angry or to the thing that made you angry.

Anger is a result of the place where you core has been pierced. Anger is the result of many things but the most important point is that anything that is worth being angry about is what you love or what you deeply care about. When you are deeply involved into something, then you are emotionally invested in that situation. What we want is to transform that same anger into action so that we can solve the problems that have led us to this point.

We aim to solve this problem in a manner such that your wrath, your revenge does not surface. Most people have the capacity to be mean, to be rude, to be disrespectful, to be unkind, to be cantankerous, to be a bully, or to be raw while speaking.

Wrath lasts. Wrath is hard to recover from. Wrath leaves a lasting mark. Wrath leaves a scorched Earth of hurt feelings and bruised egos with issues relating to the reaction to the wrath. Wrath comes in all forms. Wrath is also the cause of some irreparable damage.

As a Crown, we want to make sure that we can we cure anger gracefully and administer wrath was compassion. You want to survive this incident. That is the goal every time you are angered and your wrath forms.

Remember that you were able to be angry and you're able to have wrath but you want to make sure that when you are anger

angry and the wrath is about to ooze out, you want to still be respected as a Crown, a woman. You still want to be held high in regard with your self-esteem, and you want to let people know that you can forgive.

Time is not your friend. Time is not at your disposal. Time is not yours to control. Too many people have held grudges for too long. This is a burden. A held grudge burdens two people - you and the other person. Forgiveness is a free movement moment for you and others. Now, the time that you hold a grudge could be used to do other things such as living your best life because you or being your best self.

Time is not your friend. Are you going to be okay with someone dying while you're angry with them? If you are going to regret them dying while you were angry, then you may want to reconsider that stance. Is your anger in that wrath worth that much?

The Crown does have wrath. The Crown also needs to offer forgiveness and grace.

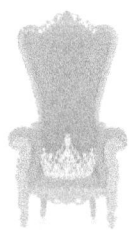

THE CROWN HAS FAITH

> ⁶ And without faith it is impossible to please God, because anyone who comes to him must believe that he exists and that he rewards those who earnestly seek him.
>
> Hebrews 11:6

The Crown has a faith that pleases God. Whew! Does she really? All the time? No. Most of the time? Probably.

Faith is the thing that separates us from those who want to be us. Faith is how we survive our lives. We live tumultuous lives. We live busy lives. We live busy lives because we manage businesses. We manage families. We manage jobs. We love. We teach. We work. We organize. We plan. We travel. We overbook. We arrived late. We worry. We experience trauma. We experience heartbreak. We overcome things that we never thought that we would.

We believed when we had no reason to do so. We have faith. Our initial faith was built on someone else's faith. A grandmother. An aunt. A mom. A mentor. We repeated what she did. We just followed in her steps. One day, we were walking alone and didn't actually realize that we had for the first time lived on the faith and it was all our own. We imitated hers, but it belonged to us.

Eventually, it was the day, that one event that required our own faith - completely all our own. An abundant faith.

This faith is intoxicating to most - those who have an equally amazing faith. While to others, our faith is confusing, completely incomprehensible. Faith is something that we can claim when our circumstances are good or mild. Faith is really tested when circumstances are fatal or near fatal. The faith that God expects from us is the faith that wins His heart over, moves Him to love, and causes Him to reconsider your situation.

Faith keeps you focused. Faith forces you toward wholeness. Faith reminds you that God is your strong tower. Faith is your action mechanism. Faith simulates a love level that is unexpected and unforeseen. Faith is a working document. Faith is a mysterious element. Faith is not applied in a consistent manner in a consistent measurement. Tuesday may need an ounce. Friday definitely needs a pound. This is something that only experience teaches us but we don't want to learn that much in the amount of experience required to arrive at the right place.

Faith is not a race, but it is about endurance. Faith is about the energy that is required to survive the situation. Faith is the belief required to overcome the unexpected stuff that will rise for the rest of your life.

Faith is experienced. Faith is learned. Faith cannot be measured in metric measurements. Faith can be seen in behavior. But faith cannot be seen. The Crown has faith. The Crown uses that faith to extend her power. The power that the Crown needs to continue being the Crown. Life is unbearable without faith.

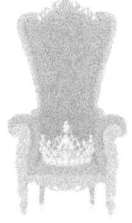

Sometimes, your faith will wane, maybe even fail you. But we can't let our faith fail us for long. We need faith to survive this life and all its elements.

Without faith, it is impossible to please God. We need faith - sometimes we want to abandon the faith we have because it does not seem to be getting us through our current situation, but if we remain steadfast, we will remain faithful. We need to figure out how to remain steady to the faith; have an unwavering faith. Unwavering faith requires time and maturity, which requires time. And experience. And decisiveness. And grit.

Faith is about grit. Faith is not about instant gratification. Faith is about the long-term lifestyle that your life requires. Faith is not optional. Faith is how Crowns live.

There will be tests of your faith. Your marriage will test your faith. Your children will test your faith. Your job will test your faith. Your friends will test your faith. Your family will test your faith. Traffic will test your faith. Your health will test your faith. Your surroundings will test your faith. There is quite a measure of things that could test your faith. The outcome of that test is the strengthening of that same faith.

Faith requires introspection, an internal reflection that requires honesty and a change in direction if you are off task. Faith is not a skill. Faith is not related to your education. Faith is not about your financial or social status. Faith is not about political affiliation or community location. Faith has nothing to do with your educational alumni network or your business network. Faith

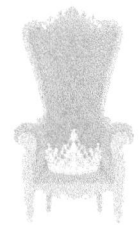

levels the playing field. Everyone can exercise their faith. Faith is not distributed like gifts or talents; everyone gets healthy, heaping portions. We need our faith. It is what we need at all times, not just in times of trouble.

Faith supports the Crown.

The Crown has faith. You want God to be pleased.

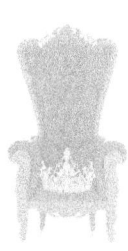

RESOURCES

Kingdom Woman   Dr. Tony Evans

With An Anointed Voice: The Power of Prayer
                                      Dr. Onedia Gage

A Woman Like Me: A Bible Study for Women to Survive Our Times   Dr. Onedia Gage

A Woman Like Me: A Daily Devotional for Women to Survive Our Times   Dr. Onedia Gage

A Woman Like Me (a sermonic study): Lessons for Us Women
                                      Dr. Onedia Gage

Yielded and Submitted: A Woman's Journey for a Life Dedicated to God   Dr. Onedia Gage

Yielded and Submitted: A Woman's Journey for a Life Dedicated to God An Intimate Study   Dr. Onedia Gage

Yielded and Submitted: A Woman's Journey for a Life Dedicated to God Prayers and Journal   Dr. Onedia Gage

Acknowledgements

God, thank You for Your plans for me. Thank You for ***With a Crown and No Home,*** and choosing me to complete Your project. I just want to please You, God. Thank You for continuing to anoint me and to invest in me and my gifts, which keep surprising me. Thank You for loving and forgiving me.

Jordan and Nehemiah, thank you for supporting me and my endeavors. Thank you for loving me, especially when I do nothing without a pen and a clipboard, thank you for enduring my late nights, your ideas, the sounding board, the love and the support. Thank you for celebrating our legacy.

To my prayer partners and to my accountability partners, thank you for the long talks and the powerful prayers and the encouragement.

To the readers who this will reach and empower and touch and affect, may these words empower you and help you reach some resolve. May you be inspired to achieve your goals and dreams. May you enhance your relationship with God so that your other relationships will also improve. May you enhance your self-esteem through prayer and study. May you have courage and peace. Share love the best you can until you can share love without reservation.

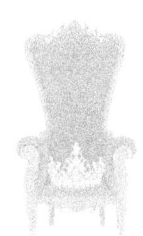

ABOUT THE SERVANT

With a Crown and No Home is extremely important for us to make a change in this world. Wear your Crown. It is necessary. Put it on so that we can fulfill our calling.

@onediangage (twitter) ♦ onediagage@onediagage.com ♦ facebook.com/onediagage

youtube.com/onediagage ♦ blogtalkradio.com/onediagage ♦ ongage (instagram)

www.coachonedia.com ♦ www.onediagagespeaks.com

Advocate ♦ Teacher ♦ Facilitator
Conference Speaker ♦ Panelist ♦ Workshop Leader

To invite Reverend Gage to speak at your Women's Conference or Bible Study,

Or other events,

Please contact us at: www.onediagagespeaks.com

@onediangage (twitter) ♦ onediagage@onediagagespeaks.com ♦ facebook.com/onediagage

youtube.com/onediagage ♦ ongage (Instagram)

Publishing

Do you have a book you want to write, but do not know what to do?

Do you have a book you need to publish but do not know how to start?

Would publishing move your career forward?

Let us help

onediagage@purpleink.net ♦ www.purpleink.net

713.705.5530 ♦ 281.740.5143

www.ingramcontent.com/pod-product-compliance
Lightning Source LLC
Chambersburg PA
CBHW061803070526
44586CB00023B/2692